Important Instruction

Students, Parents, and Teachers can use the URL or QR code provided below to access Lumos back to school refresher online assessment. Please note that this assessment is provided in the Online format only.

URL
Visit the URL below and place the book access code
http://www.lumoslearning.com/a/tedbooks
Access Code: BS89M-63478-P
OR **Scan the QR code with your Smartphone**

Lumos Back-to-School Refresher tedBook - Grade 9 Math, Back to School book to address Summer Slide designed for classroom and home use

Contributing Author   - Nicole Fernandez
Contributing Author   - Nancy Chang
Contributing Author   - Greg Applegate
Executive Producer   - Mukunda Krishnaswamy
Designer and Illustrator - Vagesh Kumar

First Edition - 2020

NGA Center/CCSSO are the sole owners and developers of the Common Core State Standards, which does not sponsor or endorse this product. © Copyright 2010. National Governors Association Center for Best Practices and Council of Chief State School Officers.

ISBN-13: 978-1-082808-53-1

Printed in the United States of America

For permissions and additional information contact us

Lumos Information Services, LLC
PO Box 1575, Piscataway, NJ 08855-1575
http://www.LumosLearning.com

Email: support@lumoslearning.com
Tel: (732) 384-0146
Fax: (866) 283-6471

Lumos Learning
Developed by Expert Teachers

Table of Contents

INTRODUCTION

This book is specifically designed to help diagnose and remedy Summer Learning Loss in students who are starting their ninth grade classes. It provides a comprehensive and efficient review of 8th Grade Math standards through an online assessment. Before starting ninth grade instruction, parents/teachers can administer this online test to their students. After the students complete the test, a standards mastery report is immediately generated to pinpoint any proficiency gaps. Using the diagnostic report and the accompanying study plan, students can get targeted remedial practice through lessons included in this book to overcome any Summer learning loss.

Addressing the Summer slide during the first few weeks of a new academic will help students have a productive ninth grade experience.

The online program also gives your student an opportunity to briefly explore various standards that are included in the 9th grade curriculum.

Some facts about Summer Learning Loss
- Students often lose an average of 2 and ½ months of math skills
- Students often lose 2 months of reading skills
- Teachers spend at least the first 4 to 5 weeks of the new school year reteaching important skills and concepts

Lumos Learning Back-To-School Refresher Methodology
The following graphic shows the key components of the Lumos back-to-school refresher program.

8th Grade Online Diagnostic Test → Record Summer Learning Loss → Remediate Summer Learning loss → Ready For Grade 9

Chapter 1
Assess Summer Learning Loss

Step 1: Assess Online Diagnostic Assessment

Use the URL and access code provided below or scan the QR code to access the Diagnostic assessment and get started. The online diagnostic test helps to measure the summer loss and remediate loss in an efficient and effective way.

After completing the test, your student will receive immediate feedback with detailed reports on standards mastery. With this report, use the next section of the book to design a practice plan for your student to overcome the summer loss.

URL	QR Code
Visit the URL below and place the book access code http://www.lumoslearning.com/a/tedbooks Access Code: BS89M-63478-P	

Step 2: Review the Personalized Study Plan Online

After you complete the online practice test, access your individualized study plan from the table of contents (Figure 2)

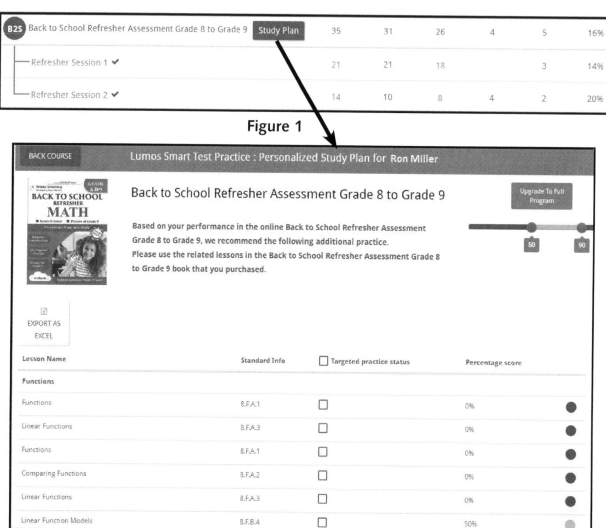

B2S Back to School Refresher Assessment Grade 8 to Grade 9	Study Plan	35	31	26	4	5	16%
Refresher Session 1 ✔		21	21	18		3	14%
Refresher Session 2 ✔		14	10	8	4	2	20%

Figure 1

BACK COURSE   Lumos Smart Test Practice : Personalized Study Plan for Ron Miller

Back to School Refresher Assessment Grade 8 to Grade 9

Upgrade To Full Program

Based on your performance in the online Back to School Refresher Assessment Grade 8 to Grade 9, we recommend the following additional practice. Please use the related lessons in the Back to School Refresher Assessment Grade 8 to Grade 9 book that you purchased.

50   90

EXPORT AS EXCEL

Lesson Name	Standard Info	☐ Targeted practice status	Percentage score	
Functions				
Functions	8.F.A.1	☐	0%	●
Linear Functions	8.F.A.3	☐	0%	●
Functions	8.F.A.1	☐	0%	●
Comparing Functions	8.F.A.2	☐	0%	●
Linear Functions	8.F.A.3	☐	0%	●
Linear Function Models	8.F.B.4	☐	50%	◐

Figure 2

Step 3: Remediate Summer Learning Loss

Using the information provided in the study plan report, complete the targeted practice using the appropriate lessons in this book to overcome Summer learning loss. Using the Lesson Name, find the appropriate practice lessons in this book and answer the questions provided. After completing the practice in the book you can mark the progress in your study plan as shown the figure 2. Please use the answer key and detailed answers provided for each lesson to gain further understanding of the learning objective.

The Number System

8.NS.A.1 Rational vs Irrational Numbers

1. The number 57 belongs to which of the following set(s) of numbers?

   Ⓐ N only
   Ⓑ N, W, and Z only
   Ⓒ N, W, Z, and Q only
   Ⓓ All of the following: N, W, Z, Q, and R

2. From the following set: $\{-\sqrt{5.7}, -9, 0, 5.25, 3i, \sqrt{16}\}$
   Select the answer choice that shows the elements which are Natural numbers.

   Ⓐ $-\sqrt{5.7}, -9, 0, 5.25, 3i, \sqrt{16}$
   Ⓑ $-\sqrt{5.7}, -9, 0, 5.25, 3i$
   Ⓒ $3i$
   Ⓓ Positive square root of 16

3. From the following set: $\{-\sqrt{5.7}, -9, 0, 5.25, 3i, \sqrt{16}\}$
   Select the answer choice that shows the elements that are Rational numbers.

   Ⓐ $-\sqrt{5.7}, -9, 0, 5.25, 3i, \sqrt{16}$
   Ⓑ $-9, 0, 5.25, \sqrt{16}$
   Ⓒ $3i$
   Ⓓ $-\sqrt{5.7}$

4. Which of the numbers below is irrational?

   Ⓐ $\sqrt{169}$
   Ⓑ $\sqrt{4}$
   Ⓒ $\sqrt{16}$
   Ⓓ $\sqrt{3}$

5. Identify the irrational number and circle it.

   Ⓐ $\dfrac{5}{7}$
   Ⓑ 0.1
   Ⓒ $\sqrt{10}$

8.NS.A.2 Approximating Irrational Numbers

1. Choose the correct order (least to greatest) for the following real numbers.

   Ⓐ $\sqrt{5}$, $4\frac{1}{2}$, 4.75, $2\sqrt{10}$

   Ⓑ $4\frac{1}{2}$, $\sqrt{5}$, $2\sqrt{10}$, 4.75

   Ⓒ $4\frac{1}{2}$, 4.75, $\sqrt{5}$, $2\sqrt{10}$

   Ⓓ $\sqrt{5}$, $2\sqrt{10}$, $4\frac{1}{2}$, 4.75

2. Which of the following numbers has the greatest value?

   Ⓐ .4...
   Ⓑ .444
   Ⓒ $\sqrt{.4}$
   Ⓓ .45

3. Which is the correct order of the following numbers when numbering from least to greatest?

   Ⓐ $\sqrt{.9}$, .9, .999, .9...
   Ⓑ .9, $\sqrt{.9}$, .999, .9...
   Ⓒ .9, .9..., $\sqrt{.9}$, .999
   Ⓓ .9, .9..., .999, $\sqrt{.9}$

4. Write the following numbers from least to greatest.

   Ⓐ $\sqrt{2}$, π, $3\frac{7}{8}$, $\frac{32}{8}$

   Ⓑ π, $\sqrt{2}$, $3\frac{7}{8}$, $\frac{32}{8}$

   Ⓒ $3\frac{7}{8}$, π, $\sqrt{2}$, $\frac{32}{8}$

   Ⓓ $\frac{32}{8}$, $3\frac{7}{8}$, π, $\sqrt{2}$

The Number System
Answer Key & Detailed Explanations

8.NS.A.1 - Rational vs. Irrational Numbers

Question No.	Answer	Detailed Explanation
1	D	The number 57 meets the requirements of each of the following sets of numbers: N (natural numbers), W (whole numbers), Z (integers), Q (rational numbers), and R (real numbers).
2	D	By definition, the natural numbers, N, are the set of counting numbers. Some mathematicians also include zero in this set. Since $\sqrt{16} = +4$ or -4 and +4 is a counting number, it is included in N. None of the choices offered 0 as an option; so, in this case, it is a mute point.
3	B	3i is an imaginary number and therefore not rational and $-\sqrt{5.7}$ cannot be expressed as a terminating or repeating decimal and consequently is not rational. Therefore, there is only one choice that does not include one or the other or both of these two numbers. Option B is the correct answer.
4	D	$\sqrt{3}$ is non-terminating and non-repeating.
5	C	$\sqrt{10}$ is the irrational number because it cannot be written as a fraction. The others can.

8.NS.A.2 - Approximating Irrational Numbers

Question No.	Answer	Detailed Explanation
1	A	$4\frac{1}{2} = 4.5$ $2 < \sqrt{5} < 3$ $\sqrt{10} > 3$; so $2\sqrt{10} > 6$ Then, the correct order is: $\sqrt{5}, 4\frac{1}{2}, 4.75, 2\sqrt{10}$
2	C	$\sqrt{.4} =$ (approx.) .63 which is the greatest of these numbers.
3	B	$\sqrt{.9} =$ (approx.) .95 So .9, $\sqrt{.9}$, .999, .9... is the correct order.
4	A	$\frac{32}{8} = 4, 3\frac{7}{8} = 3.875, \pi =$ (approx) 3.14, $\sqrt{2} =$ (approx) 1.4 The correct order is $\sqrt{2}, \pi, 3\frac{7}{8}, \frac{32}{8}$

Expressions and Equations

8.EE.A.1 Properties of Exponents

1. $1^9 =$

   Ⓐ 1
   Ⓑ 3
   Ⓒ 9
   Ⓓ $\dfrac{1}{9}$

2. $(X^{-3})(X^{-3}) =$

   Ⓐ X^6
   Ⓑ X^9
   Ⓒ $\dfrac{1}{X^6}$
   Ⓓ $\dfrac{1}{X^9}$

3. $(X^{-2})^{-7} =$

   Ⓐ X^5

   Ⓑ X^{14}

   Ⓒ $\dfrac{1}{X^5}$

   Ⓓ $\dfrac{1}{X^{14}}$

4. Simplify this expression.
   $a^7(a^8)(a)$

   Write your answer in the box below

   ┌─────────────────────────────────┐
   │   │
   │   │
   │   │
   │   │
   └─────────────────────────────────┘

8.EE.A.2 Square & Cube Roots

1. The cube root of 66 is between which two integers?

   Ⓐ 4 and 5
   Ⓑ 3 and 4
   Ⓒ 5 and 6
   Ⓓ 6 and 7

2. Which expression has the same value as $3\sqrt{144} \div \sqrt{12}$?

   Ⓐ $3\sqrt{12}$
   Ⓑ $4\sqrt{12}$
   Ⓒ $27 \div \sqrt{12}$
   Ⓓ $33 \div \sqrt{12}$

3. The cubic root of 400 lies between which two numbers?

   Ⓐ 5 and 6
   Ⓑ 6 and 7
   Ⓒ 7 and 8
   Ⓓ 8 and 9

4. Fill in the boxes to make the statement true

   $\sqrt[3]{8}$ = ☐ since ☐ × ☐ × ☐ = 8

8.EE.A.3 Scientific Notation

1. If a number expressed in scientific notation is $N \times 10^5$, how large is the number?

   Ⓐ Between 1,000 (included) and 10,000
   Ⓑ Between 10,000 (included) and 100,000
   Ⓒ Between 100,000 (included) and 1,000,000
   Ⓓ Between 1,000,000 (included) and 10,000,000

2. Red light has a wavelength of 650×10^{-9} meters. Express the wavelength in scientific notation.

   Ⓐ 65.0×10^{-10} meters
   Ⓑ 65.0×10^{-8} meters
   Ⓒ 6.50×10^{-7} meters
   Ⓓ 6.50×10^{-11} meters

3. A strand of hair from a human head is approximately 1×10^{-4} meters thick. What fraction of a meter is this?

   Ⓐ $\dfrac{1}{100}$

   Ⓑ $\dfrac{1}{1,000}$

   Ⓒ $\dfrac{1}{10,000}$

   Ⓓ $\dfrac{1}{100,000}$

4. Change 2,347,000,000 from standard form to scientific notation by filling in the blank boxes.

   ☐☐☐ × 10☐

8.EE.A.4 Solving Problems Involving Scientific Notation

1. Which of the following is **NOT** equal to $(5 \times 10^5) \times (9 \times 10^{-3})$?

    Ⓐ 4.5×10^4
    Ⓑ 4.5×10^3
    Ⓒ $4,500$
    Ⓓ 45×100

2. Find $(5 \times 10^7) \div (10 \times 10^2)$ and express the result in scientific notation.

    Ⓐ 5×10^4
    Ⓑ 0.5×10^5
    Ⓒ 50×10^9
    Ⓓ 5.0×10^9

3. Approximate $.00004567 \times .00001234$ and express the result in scientific notation.

    Ⓐ 5.636×10^{-8}
    Ⓑ 5.636×10^{-9}
    Ⓒ 5.636×10^{-10}
    Ⓓ **None of the above.**

4. Select the ones that correctly demonstrate the operations of scientific notation.

    Note that more than one option may be correct. Select all the correct answers.

    Ⓐ $(4.0 \times 10^3)(5.0 \times 10^5) = 2 \times 10^9$
    Ⓑ $\dfrac{4.5 \times 10^5}{9.0 \times 10^9} = 2 \times 10^4$

    Ⓒ $(2.1 \times 10^5) + (2.7 \times 10^5) = 4.8 \times 10^5$
    Ⓓ $(3.1 \times 10^5) - (2.7 \times 10^2) = 0.4 \times 10^3$

8.EE.B.5 Compare Proportions

1. Which statement is false?

    Ⓐ Unit cost is calculated by dividing the amount of items by the total cost.
    Ⓑ Unit cost is calculated by dividing the total cost by the amount of items.
    Ⓒ Unit cost is the cost of one unit item.
    Ⓓ On similar items, a higher unit cost is not the better price.

2. Selena is preparing for her eighth grade graduation party. She must keep within the budget set by her parents. Which is the best price for her to purchase ice cream?

    Ⓐ $3.99/ 24 oz carton
    Ⓑ $4.80/ one-quart carton
    Ⓒ $11.00 / one gallon tub
    Ⓓ $49.60/ five gallon tub

3. Ben is building a ramp for his skate boarding club. Which of the following provides the least steep ramp?

    Ⓐ 2 feet vertical for every 10 feet horizontal
    Ⓑ 3 feet vertical for every 9 feet horizontal
    Ⓒ 4 feet vertical for every 16 feet horizontal
    Ⓓ 5 feet vertical for every 30 feet horizontal

4. Solve for the proportion for the missing number.

    $$\frac{2}{7} = \frac{4}{\boxed{}}$$

    Fill in the blank box with the correct answer.

8.EE.B.6 Understanding Slope

1. Fill in the blank with one of the four choices to make the following a true statement. Knowing _____ and the y-intercept is NOT enough for us to write the equation of the line.

   Ⓐ direction
   Ⓑ a point on a given line
   Ⓒ the x-intercept
   Ⓓ the slope

2. A skateboarder is practicing at the city park. He is skating up and down the steepest straight line ramp. If the highest point on the ramp is 30 feet above the ground and the horizontal distance from the base of the ramp to a point directly beneath the upper end is 500 feet, what is the slope of the ramp?

   Ⓐ $\dfrac{500}{30}$

   Ⓑ $\dfrac{50}{3}$

   Ⓒ $\dfrac{3}{50}$

   Ⓓ None of these.

3. If the equation of a line is expressed as $y = \dfrac{3}{2} x - 9$, what is the slope of the line?

   Ⓐ - 9

   Ⓑ +9

   Ⓒ $\dfrac{3}{2}$

   Ⓓ $\dfrac{2}{3}$

4. Find the slope between the points (-12, -5) and (0, 8).

   Write your answer in the box given below.

8.EE.C.7.A Solving Linear Equations

1. Find the solution to the following equation:

    6x + 1 = 4x - 3

    Ⓐ x = -1
    Ⓑ x = -2
    Ⓒ x = - 0.5
    Ⓓ There is no solution.

2. Find the solution to the following equation:

    2x + 6 + 1 = 7 + 2x

    Ⓐ x = -3
    Ⓑ x = 3
    Ⓒ x = 7
    Ⓓ All real numbers are solutions.

3. Find the solution to the following equation:

    8x - 1 = 8x

    Ⓐ x = 7
    Ⓑ x = -8
    Ⓒ x = 8
    Ⓓ There is no solution.

4. Solve for x: 5x + 20 = -20.

    x = ?

    Write your answer in the box given below.

    ┌─────────────────────────────┐
    │   │
    │   │
    │   │
    │   │
    │   │
    └─────────────────────────────┘

8.EE.C.7.B Solve Linear Equations with Rational Numbers

1. Solve the following linear equation:

   $2(x-5) = \dfrac{1}{2}(6x+4)$

   Ⓐ x= -12
   Ⓑ x= -9
   Ⓒ x= -4
   Ⓓ There is no solution.

2. Solve the following linear equation for x.

   $3x + 2 + x = \dfrac{1}{3}(12x + 6)$

   Ⓐ x= -4
   Ⓑ x= 2
   Ⓒ There is no solution.
   Ⓓ All real values for x are correct solutions.

3. $\dfrac{1}{2}x + \dfrac{2}{3}x + 5 = \dfrac{5}{2}x + 6$

   Ⓐ $x = \dfrac{33}{4}$

   Ⓑ $x = \dfrac{1}{2}$

   Ⓒ $x = -\dfrac{3}{4}$

   Ⓓ $x = -\dfrac{6}{5}$

4. Solve the following linear equation:

   $\dfrac{8}{16} = n + \dfrac{8}{16}n$

8.EE.C.8.A Solutions to Systems of Equations

1. Use the graph, to find the solution to the following system:

$$\frac{x}{2} + \frac{y}{3} = 2$$

$$3x - 2y = 48$$

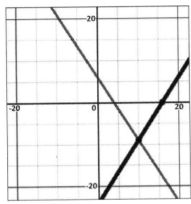

Ⓐ x = 8, y = -6
Ⓑ x = 10, y = -9
Ⓒ x = 12, y = -3
Ⓓ x = 16, y = 0

2. Which of the following best describes the relationship between the graphs of the equations in this system?

$$y = 2x - 6$$
$$y = -2x + 6$$

Ⓐ The lines intersect at the point (0, -3).
Ⓑ The lines intersect at the point (3, 0).
Ⓒ The lines do not intersect because their slopes are opposites and their y-intercepts are opposites.
Ⓓ They are the same line because their slopes are opposites and their y-intercepts are opposites.

3. Solve the system:

   2x + 3y = 14
   2x - 3y = -10

   Ⓐ x = 1, y = 4
   Ⓑ x = 2, y = 12
   Ⓒ x = 4, y = 2
   Ⓓ x = 10, y = 10

4. Randy has to raise $50.00 to repair his bicycle. He is only $1.00 short. He has only $1 and $5 bills. If he has one more $1 bills than $5 bills, how many does he have of each?

   Circle the correct answer choice.

   Ⓐ 10 $1-bills, 9 $5-bills
   Ⓑ 9 $1-bills and 8 $5-bills
   Ⓒ 8 $1-bills and 7 $5-bills
   Ⓓ 7 $1-bills and 6 $5-bills

8.EE.C.8.B Solving Systems of Equations

1. Solve the system:
   -4x + 7y = 26
   4x + 7y = 2

   ⓐ x = -3, y = 2
   ⓑ x = 3, y = -2
   ⓒ x = -2, y = 3
   ⓓ x = 2, y = -3

2. Find the solution to the following system:
   y + 3x = 11
   y - 2x = 1

   ⓐ x = -5, y = 2
   ⓑ x = 2, y = 5
   ⓒ x = -2, y = -5
   ⓓ x = -2, y = 5

3. Solve the system:
   2x + 4y = 14
   x + 2y = 7

   ⓐ x = -1, y = 4
   ⓑ x = 1, y = 3
   ⓒ There is no solution.
   ⓓ There are infinitely many solutions.

4. Fill in the table with correct solution for each system of equations.

SYSTEM	NUMBER OF SOLUTIONS
$\begin{cases} -x + 2y = 14 \\ x - 2y = -11 \end{cases}$	
$\begin{cases} 2x + 5y = 5 \\ -2x + y = -23 \end{cases}$	
$\begin{cases} y = 3x + 6 \\ -6x + 2y = 12 \end{cases}$	

8.EE.C.8.C Systems of Equations in Real-World Problems

1. Plumber A charges $50 to come to your house, plus $40 per hour of labor. Plumber B charges $75 to come to your house, plus $35 per hour of labor. If y is the total dollar amount charged for x hours of labor, which of the following systems of equations correctly represents this situation?

Ⓐ $y = 50x + 40$
$y = 75x + 35$

Ⓑ $y = 50x + 40$
$y = 35x + 75$

Ⓒ $y = 40x + 50$
$y = 75x + 35$

Ⓓ $y = 40x + 50$
$y = 35x + 75$

2. 10 tacos and 6 drinks cost $19.50. 7 tacos and 5 drinks cost $14.25. If t is the cost of one taco and d is the cost of one drink, which of the following systems of equations represents this situation?

Ⓐ $10t + 6d = 19.50$
$7t + 5d = 14.25$

Ⓑ $6t + 10d = 19.50$
$5t + 7d = 14.25$

Ⓒ $10t + 7t = 19.50$
$6d + 5d = 14.25$

Ⓓ $16(t + d) = 19.50$
$12(t + d) = 14.25$

3. Cindy has $25 saved and earns $12 per week for walking dogs. Mindy has $55 saved and earns $7 per week for watering plants. Cindy and Mindy save all of the money they earn and do not spend any of their savings. After how many weeks will they have the same amount saved? How much money will they have saved?

Ⓐ After 4 weeks, they each will have $83 saved.
Ⓑ After 5 weeks, they each will have $85 saved.
Ⓒ After 6 weeks, they each will have $97 saved.
Ⓓ After 7 weeks, they each will have $104 saved.

4. The admission fee at a carnival is $3.00 for children and $5.00 for adults. On the first day 1,500 people enter the fair and $5740 is collected. How many children and how many adults attended the carnival?

Select the correct system and answer. There can be more than one correct answer, choose all applicable ones.

Ⓐ $\begin{cases} 3c + 5a = 1500 \\ c + a = 5740 \end{cases}$

Ⓑ $\begin{cases} 3c + 5a = 5740 \\ c + a = 1500 \end{cases}$

Ⓒ $a = 620, c = 880$

Ⓓ $a = 936, c = 564$

Expressions and Equations

Answer Key
&
Detailed Explanations

8.EE.A.1 - Properties of Exponents

Question No.	Answer	Detailed Explanation
1	A	Regardless of the number of 1s that we multiply the result is always 1 because 1 is the identity element for multiplication.
2	C	When multiplying quantities with the same base, you add exponents. $(X^{-3})(X^{-3}) = X^{-6}$ To change the exponent -6 to positive 6, you write the reciprocal of X^{-6}. $\frac{1}{X^6}$
3	B	$(x^{-2})^{-7} = x^{14}$ because to raise a power to a power, we multiply exponents.
4	a^{16}	You are using your product rule to find out the exponent. When using the product rule if the base is the same, then you add the exponents. In this case, you will add $7+8+1=16$. So it would become a^{16}.

8.EE.A.2 - Square & Cube Roots

Question No.	Answer	Detailed Explanation
1	A	$4^3 = 64$ and $5^3 = 125$ Therefore, the cube root of 66 is between 4 and 5.
2	A	$3\sqrt{144} \div \sqrt{12} = 3(12) \div \sqrt{12} = (3 \times \sqrt{12} \times \sqrt{12}) \div \sqrt{12} = 3\sqrt{12}$
3	C	$7^3 = 343$ and $8^3 = 512$ Therefore, the cube root of 400 lies between 7 and 8.
4	$\sqrt[3]{8} = 2$ since $2 \times 2 \times 2 = 8$	Taking the cube root of a number is finding a number that multiplied by itself 3 times will give you the number under the radical. In this case the cuberoot of 8 will equal 2 because $2 \times 2 \times 2 = 8$.

8.EE.A.3 - Scientific Notation

Question No.	Answer	Detailed Explanation
1	C	$1 \leq N \leq 9.99...$ and we must move the decimal 5 places to the right resulting in $100,000 \leq N \times 10^5 < 1,000,000$.
2	C	To convert the given number into decimal, we must move the decimal 9 places to the left because the exponent is -9. The result is 0.000000650. Changing to scientific notation we get 6.5×10^{-7}. Or, since we must move the decimal 2 places to the left to get it properly placed for scientific notation, we only need to move it 7 more places for standard notation; so scientific notation would be written as 6.50×10^{-7}.
3	C	$1 \times 10^4 = .0001$ (By moving decimal 4 places to the left because the exponent is -4. Since the 1 is in the ten-thousandths place, the fraction will be $\dfrac{1}{10,000}$
4	2.347×10^9	The number in the first box has to be a decimal number that is larger than 1, but less than 10. In this case it will be 2.347. Next, we will take it 10 times itself to an exponent which will move our decimal until it becomes our number in standard form. So in this case we have to take 10 times itself 9 times, so our exponent will be 9. Our final answer will be $2.347 \times 10 \char`\^ 9$

8.EE.A.4 - Solving Problems Involving Scientific Notation

Question No.	Answer	Detailed Explanation
1	A	$(5 \times 10^5) \times (9 \times 10^{-3}) = (45 \times 10^{5-3}) = 45 \times 10^2 = 4.5 \times 10^3$ Therefore, 4.5×10^4 is not equal to 4.5×10^3, so 4.5×10^4 is the correct answer. Options (B), (C) and (D) are different ways of expressing the same number.
2	A	$(5 \times 10^7) \div (10 \times 10^2) = 0.5 \times 10^{(7-2)} = 0.5 \times 10^5 = 5 \times 10^4$
3	C	$.00004567 \times .00001234 = (4.567 \times 10^{-5}) \times (1.234 \times 10^{-5})$ $= (4.567 \times 1.234) \times 10^{-5 + (-5)} = 5.635678 \times 10^{-10}$ 5.636×10^{-10} is the correct answer.

Question No.	Answer	Detailed Explanation
4	A, C	$(4.0 \times 10^3)(5.0 \times 10^5) = (4 \times 5) \times (10^{3+5}) = 20 \times 10^8 = 2.0 \times 10^9$. Therefore option (A) is correct.
		$(4.5 \times 10^5) / (9.0 \times 10^9) = (45 \times 10^4)/(9 \times 10^9) = (45/9) \times 10^{4-9} = 5.0 \times 10^{-5}$. This is not equal to 2.0×10^4. Therefore, option (B) is incorrect.
		$(2.1 \times 10^5) + (2.7 \times 10^5) = (2.1 + 2.7) \times 10^5 = 4.8 \times 10^5$. Therefore option (C) is correct.
		$(3.1 \times 10^5) - (2.7 \times 10^2) = (3.1 \times 10^3 - 2.7) \times 10^2 = (3100 - 2.7) \times 10^2 = (3097.3) \times 10^2 = 3.097 \times 10^5$. This is not equal to 0.4×10^3. Therefore option (D) is incorrect.

8.EE.B.5 - Compare Proportions

Question No.	Answer	Detailed Explanation
1	A	Unit cost is calculated by dividing the total cost by the amount of items. This statement is true. Therefore, "Unit cost is calculated by dividing the amount of items by the total cost." must be a false statement. (This would represent the number of items you get per dollar paid.)
2	D	1 qt = 32 fl oz 1 gallon = 128 fl oz 5 gallons = 640 fl oz $\frac{\$3.99}{24}$ fl oz = $0.16625 per fl oz $\frac{\$4.80}{32}$ fl oz = $0.15 per fl oz $\frac{\$11.00}{128}$ fl oz = $0.0859375 per fl oz $\frac{\$49.60}{640}$ fl oz = $0.0775 per fl oz--- So, the five gallon tub offers the best price
3	D	$\frac{5 \text{ ft}}{30 \text{ ft}} = \frac{1}{6}$ which is the least steep slope
4	y=14	To solve this proportion you will have to use cross products. You will multiply the numerator of one to the denominator of the other and the denomiator of the first to the numerator of the second. In this case we would have 7x4=2y. So 28=2y. Next you want to get the variable alone, so you have to use inverse operations to move the 2. In this case we will divide both sides by 2. Thus leaving us with y=14.

8.EE.B.6 - Understanding Slope

Question No.	Answer	Detailed Explanation
1	A	If we know the y-intercept and the slope, we can write the equation of a straight line. If we know the y-intercept, we know b in the slope-intercept formula. The y-intercept together with another point or the x-intercept make it possible to determine the slope of the line. Direction would not give enough information.
2	C	Slope = rise/run (vertical change/horizontal change) Slope = $\dfrac{30}{500} = \dfrac{3}{50}$
3	C	$y = mx + b$ $m = $ slope In this case, we have $y = (\dfrac{3}{2})x - 9$ so $m = \dfrac{3}{2}$
4	The slope is $\dfrac{13}{12}$	To find the slope between 2 ordered pairs you use the formula $\dfrac{y_2 - y_1}{x_2 - x_1}$ This would look like $\dfrac{8-(-5)}{0-(-12)} = \dfrac{13}{12}$ So the slope between the two points is $\dfrac{13}{12}$

8.EE.C.7.A - Solving Linear Equations

Question No.	Answer	Detailed Explanation
1	B	6x + 1 = 4x - 3 6x - 4x = - 3 - 1 2x = - 4 $x = -\dfrac{4}{2}$ x = -2
2	D	2(x + 3) + 1 = 7 + 2x 2x + 6 + 1 = 7 + 2x 2x + 7 = 7 + 2x Since both sides of the equation are identical, any real solution satisfies the equation.
3	D	8x - 1 = 8x -1 = 0 Since this is a false statement, there is no solution to this equation.
4	-8	To solve this 2-step equation you must first get rid of the 20. Since it is adding 20, to undo it you must subtract 20 from both sides. Making it now 5x=-40. Now the second step is to undo the multiplication. To undo it, we will divide both sides by 5. Ending up with x=-8.

8.EE.C.7.B - Solve Linear Equations with Rational Numbers

Question No.	Answer	Detailed Explanation
1	A	$2(x-5) = \frac{1}{2}(6x + 4)$ $2x - 10 = 3x + 2$ $-12 = x$
2	D	$3x + 2 + x = \frac{1}{3}(12x + 6)$ $3x + x + 2 = 4x + 2$ $4x + 2 = 4x + 2$ $0 = 0$ Thus, all real values of x are correct solutions.
3	C	$\frac{1}{2}x + \frac{2}{3}x + 5 = \frac{5}{2}x + 6$ $6(\frac{1}{2}x + \frac{2}{3}x + 5 = \frac{5}{2}x + 6)$ $3x + 4x + 30 = 15x + 36$ $-8x = 6$ $x = -\frac{6}{8} = -\frac{3}{4}$
4	$n = \frac{1}{3}$	$\frac{8}{16} = n + \frac{8}{16}n$ Multiplying both sides by 2, we get, $2 \times \frac{8}{16} = = 2(n + \frac{8}{16}n)$ $1 = 2n + n$ $3n = 1$ Therefore, $n = \frac{1}{3}$

8.EE.C.8.A - Solutions to Systems of Equations

Question No.	Answer	Detailed Explanation
1	B	The given equations represent two straight lines and the point of intersection of these lines will be the solution of these equations. By looking at the graph, the point of intersection is (10, -9). Therefore, option B is the correct answer.
2	B	y = 2x - 6 y = -2x + 6 2x - 6 = - 2x + 6 2x + 2x = 6 + 6 4x = 12 x = 3 y = 2(3) -6 = 0
3	A	Adding the two equations, we get 4x = 4; x =1 Then substituting into 2x + 3y = 14, we get 2 + 3y = 14 3y = 14 - 2 3y = 12 y = 4
4	B	Let x = the number of $1 bills that he has. Let y = the number of $5 bills that he has. x + 5y = 49 (Eq. 1) x = y + 1 x - y = 1. Multiplying this equation by 5, we get 5x - 5y = 5 (Eq. 2) Adding Eq. 1 and Eq. 2, 6x = 54 x = 9 ($1 bills) Substitutine x = 9 in x - y = 1, we get, y = 8 ($5 bills)

8.EE.C.8.B - Solving Systems of Equations

Question No.	Answer	Detailed Explanation
1	A	Adding the two equations, we get $14y = 28$. $y = 2$ Substituting into $4x + 7y = 2$, we get $4x + 14 = 2$ $4x = -12$ $x = -3$
2	B	$y + 3x = 11$ $y - 2x = 1$ Multiplying the $(y + 3x = 11)$ by 2 and $(y - 2x = 1)$ by 3 we get $2y + 6x = 22$ Eq. 1 $3y - 6x = 3$ Eq. 2 Adding Eq. 1 and Eq. 2, $5y = 25$ $y = 5$; Substituting $y = 5$ in $y - 2x = 1$ $5 - 2x = 1$; $-2x = 1-5 = -4$ $2x = 4$ $x = 2$
3	D	$2x + 4y = 14$ $x + 2y = 7$ Dividing the first equation by 2, we get the second equation. Therefore, there are an infinite number of solutions.
4	No Solution, One Soultion & Infinite Solution.	The first one has no solution because if you rearrange these into slope intercept form, you will see that they both have the same slope but different y - intercept. If they have the same slope and different y - intercept, they will be parallel and do not intersect. The second one has one solution because if you solve the system you will end up with one value for x and y, giving you the ordered pair where they intersect. The last one will have infinite solutions because if you take out a factor of 2 from $-6x + 2y = 12$ and rearrange them both to slope intercept form you will see that they are the exact same line which means they will intersect at every point.

8.EE.C.8.C - Systems of Equations in Real-World Problems

Question No.	Answer	Detailed Explanation
1	D	Total cost for Plumber A is 40x + 50 and for Plumber B is 35x + 75.
2	A	10t + 6d = 19.50 7t + 5d = 14.25 correctly expresses the relative costs as described.
3	C	Let C = money Cindy has. Let M = money Mindy has. C = 25 + 12w where w is the weeks worked. M = 55 + 7w where w is the weeks worked. 25 +12w = 55 + 7w ; 12w - 7w = 55 - 25 5w = 30 ; w = 6 weeks ; C = 25 + 12(6) = $97.00 M = 55 + 7(6) = $97.00
4	B, C	1500 people enter the fair which includes children and adults and can be represented by c+a=1500. The admission fee is $3 for children and $5 for adults. So 3c+5a=5740 would represent the total fair collected. Hence option B is the correct answer. Solving these equations will give us a=620 and c=880. Therefore, option C is also the correct answer.

Functions

8.F.A.1 Functions

1. Which of the following is true of the graph of any non-constant function?

    Ⓐ A line drawn parallel to the x-axis will never cross the graph.
    Ⓑ A line drawn perpendicular to the x-axis will never cross the graph.
    Ⓒ A line drawn through the graph parallel to the x-axis will cross the graph one and only one time.
    Ⓓ A line drawn through the graph perpendicular to the x-axis will cross the graph one and only one time.

2. The given set represents a function:
    {(0,1), (1,1), (2,1)}
    If the ordered pair ____ was added to the set, it would no longer be a function.

    Ⓐ (3,1)
    Ⓑ (3,2)
    Ⓒ (3,3)
    Ⓓ (2,3)

3. In order for this set, {(6,5), (5,4), (4,3)}, to remain a function, which of the following ordered pairs COULD be added to it?

    Ⓐ (6,6)
    Ⓑ (5,5)
    Ⓒ (4,4)
    Ⓓ (3,3)

4. Write the function that would go with the table.

x	2	3	4	5
y	-1	0	1	2

8.F.A.2 Comparing Functions

1. The graph of linear function A passes through the point (5, 6). The graph of linear function B passes through the point (6, 7). The two graphs intersect at the point (2, 5). Which of the following statements is true?

   Ⓐ Function A has the greater slope.
   Ⓑ Both functions have the same slope.
   Ⓒ Function B has the greater slope.
   Ⓓ No relationship between the slopes of the lines can be determined from this information.

2. If line M includes the points (-1, 4) and (7, 9) and line N includes the points (5, 2) and (-3, -3), which of the following describes the relationship between M and N?

   Ⓐ They are perpendicular.
   Ⓑ They intersect but are not perpendicular.
   Ⓒ They are parallel.
   Ⓓ Not enough information is provided.

3. If line R includes the points (-2, -2) and (6, 4) and line S includes the points(0,4) and (3,0) which of the following describes the relationship between R and S?

   Ⓐ They are perpendicular.
   Ⓑ They intersect but are not perpendicular.
   Ⓒ They are parallel.
   Ⓓ Not enough information is provided.

4. Put the correct inequality or equality sign between the rates of change of the two functions given below.

   Instruction : Take f to be the first function {(0, 0), (3, 180), (6, 360), (9, 540)} and g to be the second function y = 100x

   {(0, 0), (3, 180), (6, 360), (9, 540)} [ ] y = 100x

8.F.A.3 Linear Functions

1. Four (x, y) pairs of a certain function are shown in the table below. Which of the following statement describes the function correctly?

x	y
0	3
1	4
2	7
3	12

Ⓐ The function is linear because it does not include the point (0, 0).
Ⓑ The function is linear because it does not have the same slope between different pairs of points.
Ⓒ The function is nonlinear because it does not include the point (0, 0).
Ⓓ The function is nonlinear because it does not have the same slope between different pairs of points.

2. The graph of a linear function lies in the first and fourth quadrants. Which of the following CANNOT be true?

Ⓐ It is an increasing function.
Ⓑ It is a constant function.
Ⓒ It also lies in the second quadrant.
Ⓓ It also lies in the third quadrant.

3. A linear function includes the ordered pairs (0, 1), (3, 3), and (9, n). What is the value of n?

Ⓐ 5
Ⓑ 6
Ⓒ 7
Ⓓ 8

4. Write whether this represents a linear or non-linear function.

$2x^2 + 3y = 10$

8.F.B.4 Linear Function Models

1. A young child is building a tower of blocks on top of a bench. The bench is 18 inches high, and each block is 3 inches high. Which of the following functions correctly relates the total height of the tower (including the bench) h, in inches, to the number of blocks b?

   Ⓐ h = 3b - 18
   Ⓑ h = 3b + 18
   Ⓒ h = 18b - 3
   Ⓓ h = 18b + 3

2. Jim owes his parents $10. Each week, his parents pay him $5 for doing chores. Assuming that Jim does not earn money from any other source and does not spend any of his money. Which of the following functions correctly relates the total amount of money m, in dollars, that Jim will have to the number of weeks w?

   Ⓐ m = -5w - 10
   Ⓑ m = -5w + 10
   Ⓒ m = 5w - 10
   Ⓓ m = 5w + 10

3. An amusement park charges $5 admission and an additional $2 per ride. Which of the following functions correctly relates the total amount paid p, in dollars, to the number of rides, r?

   Ⓐ p = 2r + 5
   Ⓑ p = 5r + 2
   Ⓒ p = 10r
   Ⓓ p = 7r

4. A cell phone company charges $89.99 for a new phone and then $19.99 per month. What is the slope or rate of change for this situation?

   Slope = _____

8.F.B.5 Analyzing Functions

1. A linear equation is plotted on the coordinate plane, and its graph is perpendicular to the x-axis. Which of the following best describes the slope of this line?

   Ⓐ Zero
   Ⓑ Undefined
   Ⓒ Negative
   Ⓓ Positive

2. The graph of a decreasing linear function crosses the vertical axis at (0, 3). Which of the following CANNOT be true?

   Ⓐ The graph lies in the first quadrant.
   Ⓑ The graph lies in the second quadrant.
   Ⓒ The graph lies in the third quadrant.
   Ⓓ The graph lies in the fourth quadrant.

3. Which of the following best describes the x & y coordinates of any point in the first quadrant?

   Ⓐ Both are positive
   Ⓑ Both are negative
   Ⓒ One is positive and one is negative
   Ⓓ None of these

4. Match each equation with whether or not the function is increasing, decreasing, or constant.

	INCREASING	DECREASING	CONSTANT
$y=-2x+5$	○	○	○
$y=6$	○	○	○
$y=-\frac{1}{2}x$	○	○	○
$y=5x-9$	○	○	○

Functions

Answer Key
&
Detailed Explanations

8.F.A.1 - Functions

Question No.	Answer	Detailed Explanation
1	D	A line drawn through the graph perpendicular to the x-axis will cross the graph one and only one time because, for each value of x, there will be one and only one value of y.
2	D	In a function, for each value of x, there must be one and only one value for y. We already have (2,1) so cannot have another ordered pair where x=2.
3	D	There is already an assigned y value for x=6, x=5, and x=4, but not for x = 3.
4	y=x-3	The rule for this function is y=x-3. To get this you find the slope first. In this case the slope is 1. Then you find out when the y is zero. In this case it is when x is 3. Thus combining them to form the rule.

8.F.A.2 - Comparing Functions

Question No.	Answer	Detailed Explanation
1	C	Function A has a slope of $\frac{1}{3}$ and Function B has a slope of $\frac{1}{2}$. Therefore, Function B has a greater slope. To verify, apply the formula: Slope = $m = (y_2-y_1)/(x_2-x_1)$ to each function.
2	C	The slope (m) of Line A $= \frac{9-4}{7-(-1)} = \frac{5}{8}$ The slope (m) of Line B $= \frac{-3-2}{-3-5} = \frac{-5}{-8} = \frac{5}{8}$ Since their slopes are equal, the lines are parallel.
3	A	The slope (m) of Line R $= \frac{4+2}{6+2} = \frac{6}{8} = \frac{3}{4}$ The slope (m) of Line S $= \frac{4-0}{0-3} = \frac{4}{-3}$ Since their slopes are negative reciprocals of each other, the lines are perpendicular.
4	Rate of change of function f< [Rate of change of function g]	For the function y = 100x, you know the rate of change is 100, so you need to find out the rate of change of the other one. To do this you will have to find the slope, $\frac{180-0}{3-0}$ which is equal to 60. So in this case we are comparing 60 and 100. Since 60 is smaller than 100 the inequality symbol should be < (less than) for this situation.

8.F.A.3 - Linear Functions

Question No.	Answer	Detailed Explanation
1	D	Only the last statement, the function is nonlinear because it does not have the same slope between different pairs of points, is true.
2	B	If it is a function, x has to change as y changes, but if that is true, the line cannot be constant for y unless it is in quadrants I and II, or III and IV, or it is the x-axis.
3	C	If the function is linear, the slope has to be the same between any 2 points. Using the first two points, the slope is $\frac{2}{3}$. Therefore, using the next two points, the slope must also be $\frac{2}{3}$; so $\frac{n-3}{9-3} = \frac{2}{3}$; so $3n-9=18-6$ $3n=12+9=21$ $n=7$
4	Non Linear	This function will be non-linear because if we rearrange to solve for y, you will still have x to the second power. Thus making it non-linear.

8.F.B.4 - Linear Function Models

Question No.	Answer	Detailed Explanation
1	B	The height of the bench is 18 in. and the height of one block is 3 in. So height of b blocks will be 3b in. Hence, the total height h = 3b + 18
2	C	He starts out $10 in debt so b = -10. At any point, he has earned 5w where w is the number of weeks. Therefore, m = 5w -10.
3	A	A guest must pay $5 admission before any rides; so b=5. He pays $2 per ride so the total paid in rides is 2r. Now add these two amounts and p = 2r + 5
4	$19.99	In this case the slope or rate of change is $19.99.

8.F.B.5 - Analyzing Functions

Question No.	Answer	Detailed Explanation
1	B	m = change in y / change in x. In this case change in x is 0. Division by 0 is undefined.
2	C	The graph cannot lie in the third quadrant.
3	A	In the first quadrant, both x and y are positive.
4		

	INCREASING	DECREASING	CONSTANT
$y=-2x+5$	○	●	○
$y=6$	○	○	●
$y=-\frac{1}{2}x$	○	●	○
$y=5x-9$	●	○	○

When looking at just equations, you will have to look at the slope of the line to determine whether it is increasing, decreasing, or constant. The slope is the number that is paired with the x-value. If the slope is negative, then it is decreasing. If the slope is positive, the function is increasing. If there is no slope, then the line is horizontal, making the function a constant.

Geometry

8.G.A.1 Transformations of Points & Lines

1. A line segment with end points (1, 1) and (5, 5) is moved and the new end points are now (1, 5) and (5,1). Which transformation took place?

   (A) reflection
   (B) rotation
   (C) translation
   (D) dilation

2. A certain transformation moves a line segment as follows: A (2, 1) moves to A' (2, -1) and B (5, 3) to B' (5, -3).
   Name this transformation.

   (A) Rotation
   (B) Translation
   (C) Reflection
   (D) Dilation

3. After a certain transformation is applied to point (x, y), it moves to (y, -x).
   Name the transformation.

   (A) Rotation
   (B) Translation
   (C) Reflection
   (D) Dilation

4. Enter the correct operation that will describe the rule for the translation left 3 units and up 4 units?

   (x,y) --> (x ☐ 3, y ☐ 4)

8.G.A.1.B Transformations of Angles

1. A company is looking to design a new logo, which consists only of transformations of the angle below:

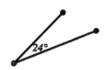

Which logo meets the company's demand?

Ⓐ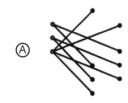

Ⓑ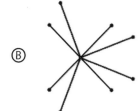

Ⓒ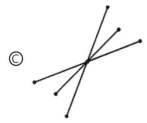

Ⓓ **All of the above**

2. The angle ∠ AOB is 45° and has been rotated 120° around point C. What is the measure of the new angle ∠ XYZ?

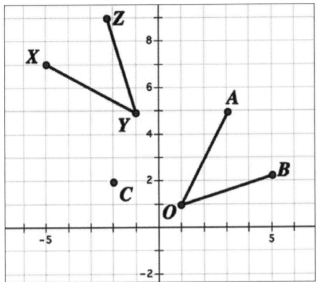

Ⓐ 30°
Ⓑ 45°
Ⓒ 90°
Ⓓ 120°

3. Find the measure of ∠ ABC

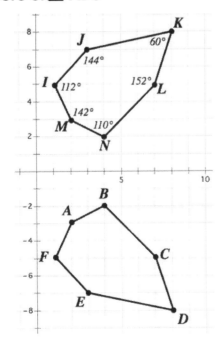

Ⓐ 110°
Ⓑ 112°
Ⓒ 142°
Ⓓ 144°

4. **Select the angle measure that corresponds with each transformation. Your preimage has an angle measure of 30°.**

	30°	60°	90°
Translation	○	○	○
Reflection	○	○	○
Rotation	○	○	○
Dilation	○	○	○

8.G.A.1.C Transformations of Parallel Lines

1. Line *L* is translated along segment $\overline{AB}$ to create line *L'*. Will *L* and *L'* ever intersect?

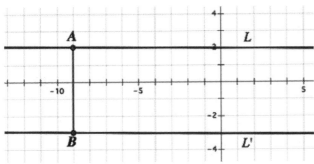

Ⓐ Yes, line *L'* is now the same as *L*.
Ⓑ Yes, parallel lines always eventually intersect.
Ⓒ No, every point on *L'* will always have a corresponding point the distance of $\overline{AB}$ away from *L'*.
Ⓓ No, the translation along $\overline{AB}$ does not change the slope from *L* to *L'*, and lines with the same slope never intersect.

2. Line *L* is translated along segement $\overline{AB}$ to create line *L'*. Will *L* and *L'* ever intersect?

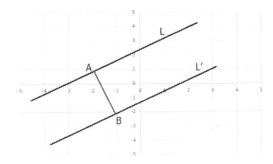

Ⓐ Yes, line *L'* is now the same as *L*.
Ⓑ Yes, parallel lines always eventually intersect.
Ⓒ Yes, every point on *L'* will not always have a corresponding point the distance of AB away from *L'*.
Ⓓ No, the translation along the line segment *AB* does not change the slope from *L* to *L'*, and lines with the same slope never intersect.

3. Line *L* is translated along ray *AC* to create line *L'*. What do you know about the relationship between line *L* and *L'*?

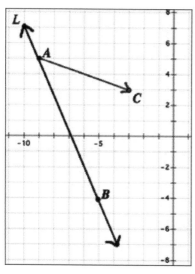

Ⓐ The lines intersect at least once.
Ⓑ The lines are exactly the same.
Ⓒ The lines are parallel.
Ⓓ None of the above.

4. Select what concepts are preserved under these different transformations. Select all that apply.

	Lengths of sides	Angle Measures	Parallel Sides on Figure
Translation	○	○	○
Reflection	○	○	○
Rotation	○	○	○
Dilation	○	○	○

8.G.A.2 Transformations of Congruency

1. **What is NOT true about the graph below?**

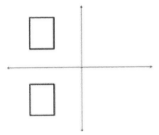

Ⓐ The object in quadrant 3 could not be a reflection of the object in quadrant 2.
Ⓑ The object in quadrant 3 could be a translation of the object in quadrant 2.
Ⓒ The two objects are congruent.
Ⓓ The object in quadrant 3 could not be a dilation of the object in quadrant 2.

2. **Finish the statement. Two congruent objects _____.**

Ⓐ have the same dimensions.
Ⓑ have different measured angles.
Ⓒ are not the same shape.
Ⓓ only apply to two-dimensional objects.

3. **What transformations can be applied to an object to create a congruent object?**

Ⓐ all transformations
Ⓑ dilation and rotation
Ⓒ translation and dilation
Ⓓ reflection, translation, and rotation

4. **Quadrilateral ABCD is translated 5 units to the left and 4 units down. Which congruent quadrilateral match this transformation?**

Write your answer in the box given below

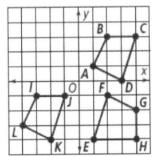

8.G.A.3 Analyzing Transformations

1. Which of the following transformations does NOT preserve congruency?

    Ⓐ Rotation
    Ⓑ Translation
    Ⓒ Reflection
    Ⓓ Dilation

2. Consider the triangle with vertices (1, 0), (2, 5) and (-1, 5). Find the vertices of the new triangle after a reflection over the vertical axis followed by a reflection over the horizontal axis.

    Ⓐ (-1, 0), (1, 5) and (-2, 5)
    Ⓑ (-1, 0), (-2, -5) and (1, -5)
    Ⓒ (1, 0), (-2, 5) and (1, 5)
    Ⓓ (1, 0), (-2, -5) and (1, -5)

3. Translate the triangle with vertices (1, 0), (2, 5), and (-1, 5), 3 units to the left. Which of the following ordered pairs represent the vertices of the new triangle?

    Ⓐ (-2, 0), (-4, 5) and (-1, 5)
    Ⓑ (4, 0), (5, 5) and (2, 5)
    Ⓒ (-1, 2), (2, 2) and (1, -3)
    Ⓓ (-1, 8), (2, 8) and (1, 3)

4. Select the coordinates that will correspond with each transformation for point A.

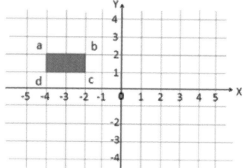

	A(4,-2)	A(-2,1)	A(-4,-2)
Translation (x+2,y-1)	○	○	○
Rotation 180°	○	○	○
Reflection over x-axis	○	○	○

LumosLearning.com

8.G.A.4 Transformations of Similarity

1. **Which graph represents reflection over an axis and dilation?**

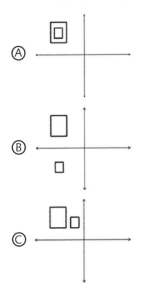

Ⓐ

Ⓑ

Ⓒ

Ⓓ **None of the above.**

2. **What transformation is necessary to have two similar, but not congruent, objects?**

Ⓐ Rotation
Ⓑ Translation
Ⓒ Dilation
Ⓓ Reflection

3. **Finish this statement. Two similar objects _____.**

Ⓐ have proportional dimensions.
Ⓑ are always congruent.
Ⓒ have different measured angles.
Ⓓ can be different shapes.

4. **The 2 figures are similar. What is the height of the 2nd figure? Write your answer in the box below.**

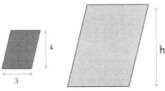

8.G.A.5 Interior & Exterior Angles in Geometric Figures

1. Two angles in a triangle measure 65° each. What is the measure of the third angle in the triangle?

   Ⓐ 25°
   Ⓑ 50°
   Ⓒ 65°
   Ⓓ 130°

2.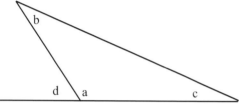

   If b = 40° and c = 30°, what is the measure of d?

   Ⓐ 35°
   Ⓑ 70°
   Ⓒ 110°
   Ⓓ 145°

3. In right triangle ABC, Angle C is the right angle. Angle A measures 70°. Find the measure of the exterior angle at angle C.

   Ⓐ 180°
   Ⓑ 90°
   Ⓒ 110°
   Ⓓ 160°

4. Match the figure with the sum of the interior angles of each polygon.

	2520	1080	1440	4140	540
Decagon	○	○	○	○	○
16-gon	○	○	○	○	○
Pentagon	○	○	○	○	○
25-gon	○	○	○	○	○
Octagon	○	○	○	○	○

8.G.B.6 Verifying the Pythagorean Theorem

1. Which of the following **INCORRECTLY** completes this statement of the Pythagorean theorem?
   In a right triangle with legs of lengths a and b and hypotenuse of length c, ...

   (A) $a^2 + b^2 = c^2$
   (B) $c^2 - a^2 = b^2$
   (C) $c^2 - b^2 = a^2$
   (D) $a^2 + c^2 = b^2$

2. A Pythagorean triple is a set of three positive integers a, b, and c that satisfy the equation $a^2 + b^2 = c^2$. Which of the following is a Pythagorean triple?

   (A) $a = 3, b = 6, c = 9$
   (B) $a = 6, b = 9, c = 12$
   (C) $a = 9, b = 12, c = 15$
   (D) $a = 12, b = 15, c = 18$

3. If an isosceles right triangle has legs of 4 inches each, find the length of the hypotenuse.

   (A) Approximately 6 in.
   (B) Approximately 5 in.
   (C) Approximately 4 in.
   (D) Approximately 3 in.

4. You have a right triangle with leg lengths of 6 and 8. What is the length of the hypotenuse? Fill in the numbers into the equation and solve.

   $6^2 + 8^2 = C^2$
   $100 = C^2$
   $\sqrt{100} = C$
   $C = ?$

8.G.B.7 Pythagorean Theorem in Real-World Problems

1. An unofficial baseball diamond is measured to be 50 yards wide. What is the approximate measurement of one side (a) of the diamond?

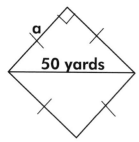

   Ⓐ 34 ft
   Ⓑ 35 yards
   Ⓒ 35 ft
   Ⓓ 36 yards

2. The neighborhood swimming pool is 20 ft wide and 30 ft long. What is the approximate measurement of the diagonal (d) of the base of the pool?

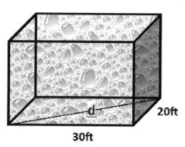

   Ⓐ 36 ft
   Ⓑ 35 ft
   Ⓒ 34 ft
   Ⓓ 34 yards

3. To get to her friend's house, a student must walk 20 feet to the corner of their streets, turn left and walk 15 feet to her friend's house.
   How much shorter would it be if she could cut across a neighbor's yard and walk a straight line from her house to her friend's house?

   Ⓐ 5 feet shorter
   Ⓑ 10 feet shorter
   Ⓒ 25 feet shorter
   Ⓓ 35 feet shorter

4. Fill in the missing information needed to solve for the word problem. Round to the nearest tenth if necessary.

WORD PROBLEM	LEG(a)	LEG(b)	HYPOTENUSE(c)
Find the height of a pyramid whose slant height is 26 cm and base length is 48 cm	24		
Find the base length of a pyramid whose height is 8 in and slant height 17 in.		8	17
The foot of a ladder is put 5 feet from the wall. If the top of the ladder is 10 feet from the ground, how long is the ladder?		10	

8.G.B.8 Pythagorean Theorem & Coordinate System

1. Find the distance (approximately) between Pt P (5, 3) and the origin (0, 0).

   Ⓐ 4.0
   Ⓑ 5.1
   Ⓒ 5.8
   Ⓓ 8.0

2. Find the distance (approximately) between the points A (11, 12) and B (7, 8).

   Ⓐ 4.0
   Ⓑ 5.3
   Ⓒ 5.7
   Ⓓ 8.0

3. Is it closer to go from Pt A (4, 6) to Pt B (2, -4) or Pt A to Pt C (-5, 2)?

   Ⓐ A to B
   Ⓑ A to C
   Ⓒ Neither, they are both the same distance.
   Ⓓ Not enough information.

4. Match the ordered pairs with the approximate distance between them.

	10.8	12.2	13	14.8
(6, 5) and (-4, 9)	○	○	○	○
(-8, 0) and (5, -7)	○	○	○	○
(-4, -9) and (6, -2)	○	○	○	○
(5, 4) and (12, 15)	○	○	○	○

8.G.C.9 Finding Volume: Cone, Cylinder, & Sphere

1. A cylinder and a cone have the same radius and the same volume. **How do the heights compare?**

   Ⓐ The height of the cylinder is 3 times the height of the cone.
   Ⓑ The height of the cylinder is 2 times the height of the cone.
   Ⓒ The height of the cone is 2 times the height of the cylinder.
   Ⓓ The height of the cone is 3 times the height of the cylinder.

2. Which of the following has the greatest volume?

   Ⓐ A sphere with a radius of 2 cm
   Ⓑ A cylinder with a height of 2 cm and a radius of 2 cm
   Ⓒ A cone with a height of 4 cm and a radius of 3 cm
   Ⓓ All three volumes are equal

3. Which of the following has the greatest volume?

   Ⓐ A sphere with a radius of 3 cm
   Ⓑ A cylinder with a height of 4 cm and a radius of 3 cm
   Ⓒ A cone with a height of 3 cm and a radius of 6 cm
   Ⓓ All three volumes are equal

4. Find the volume of the figure below. Use pi = 3.14. Write your answer in the box below.

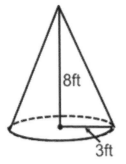

8ft

3ft

Geometry

Answer Key
&
Detailed Explanations

8.G.A.1 - Transformations of Points & Lines

Question No.	Answer	Detailed Explanation
1	B	This is a rotation, since the segment is still the same length, it is just oriented differently.
2	C	This is a reflection across the x-axis, since the x-coordinates are remaining unchanged and the y-coordinates are switching sign.
3	A	This would be a rotation through 90° clockwise.
4	x-3; y+4	In this case since you are translating left, you will need to put a subtraction sign in the first box. In the second box, since you are moving up, you will need to put an addition sign in there.

8.G.A.1.B - Transformations of Angles

Question No.	Answer	Detailed Explanation
1	D	Correct Anser: Option (D) All of the logos are a result of only reflection, rotation, or translation. Therefore, all the logos would be acceptable.
2	B	All figures that undergo rigid transformations have corresponding angles that maintain congruency. Since angle AOB corresponds to angle XYZ, the two are congruent and therefore both 45 degrees.
3	A	Correct Answer: Option (A) Corresponding angles are congruent under rigid transformations. Since figure ABCDEF is a reflected image of figure IJKLMN, and angle ABC corresponds to angle MNL, the two angles are congruent and therefore both measure 110 degrees.
4		

	30°	60°	90°
Translation	●	○	○
Reflection	●	○	○
Rotation	●	○	○
Dilation	●	○	○

Angle measures will stay the same no matter what transformation it undergoes.

8.G.A.1.C - Transformations of Parallel Lines

Question No.	Answer	Detailed Explanation
1	D	When a line is translated along a vector, the resulting line is parallel.
2	D	When a line is translated along a vector, the resulting line is parallel.
3	C	When a line is translated along a vector, the resulting line is parallel.
4		

	Lengths of sides	Angle Measures	Parallel Sides on Figure
Translation	●	●	●
Reflection	●	●	●
Rotation	●	●	●
Dilation	○	●	●

All of the transformations will preserve the angle measures. Parallel sides of the figure is also preserved i.e. parallel lines reamain parallel under all the transformations. Lengths of the sides will change when a figure undergoes a dilation. In other three transformations, lengths of sides is also preserved.

These are all properties of these different transformations. All of them will preserve the angle measures and whether or not the parallel sides will stay parallel. The only thing that they all don't have is that the side lengths will change when a figure undergoes a dilation.

8.G.A.2 - Transformations of Congruency

Question No.	Answer	Detailed Explanation
1	A	The object in quadrant III could be a reflection of the object in quadrant II. Therefore, option (A) is the correct answer.
2	A	Two congruent objects are identical and consequently have the same dimensions.
3	D	Only dilation does not preserve congruency.
4	IJKL	If you apply the transformation to the original figure you will see that quadrilater ABCD will land directly on top of quadrilateral IJKL. This will also show that the quadrilaterals will be congruent.

8.G.A.3 - Analyzing Transformations

Question No.	Answer	Detailed Explanation
1	D	Dilation does not preserve congruency.
2	B	A point (x, y) reflected in the vertical axis becomes (-x, y). A point (- x, y) reflected in the horizontal axis would become (-x, -y).
3	A	When translating a point (x, y) 3 units to the left, it will be located at (x-3, y).

4				

	A(4,-2)	A(-2,1)	A(-4,-2)
Translation (x+2,y-1)	○	●	○
Rotation 180°	●	○	○
Reflection over x-axis	○	○	●

By applying each one of the transformations to the pre-image, you can come up with the ordered pair for point A. If you translate the original point (-4,2) 2 to the right and one down you end up with (-2,1). If it is a 180 degree rotation you take the opposite of your x-coordinate and the opposite of the y-coordinate. Thus ending up with (4,-2). Finally, if it is a reflection over the x-axis your x-coordinate stays the same and you take the opposite of your y-coordinate. Thus ending up with (-4,-2).

8.G.A.4 - Transformations & Similarity

Question No.	Answer	Detailed Explanation
1	B	In the second choice, the larger object was reflected across the horizontal axis and dilated.
2	C	In order to have two similar objects, we must have a dilation.
3	A	One condition of similarity is that all dimensions are proportional.
4	8	Since the two figures are similar, you can either figure out the scale factor between them or set up a proportion. If you set up a proportion it would look like 3/6 = 4/h. Then you cross multiply and solve. Otherwise, if you look at similar parts, you can figure out how you get from one to the other. In this case you will multiply the left figure by 2 to get the right figure. So in this case h=8.

8.G.A.5 - Interior & Exterior Angles in Geometric Figures

Question No.	Answer	Detailed Explanation
1	B	a + b + c = 180° 65° + 65° + c = 180° 130° + c = 180° c = 50°
2	B	a + b + c = 180° a + 40° + 30° = 180° a = 110° a + d = 180° 110° + d = 180° d = 70° Also, the measure of an exterior angle of a triangle is equal to the sum of the measures of the two non-adjacent interior angles.
3	B	An interior angle of a triangle and its exterior angle are supplementary.

4

	2520	1080	1440	4140	540
Decagon	○	○	●	○	○
16-gon	●	○	○	○	○
Pentagon	○	○	○	○	●
25-gon	○	○	○	●	○
Octagon	○	●	○	○	○

To find the sum of the interior angles of a polygon, you use the formula the number of sides minus 2 times 180. If n is the number of sides (or interior angles), then sum of the interior angles of the polygon = (n - 2) x 180°.

(1) For Decagon, n = 10, sum of the interior angles = (10 - 2) x 180° = 1440°

(2) For 16-gon, n = 16, sum of the interior angles = (16 - 2) x 180° = 2520°

(3) For Pentagon, n = 5. sum of the interior angles = (5 - 2) x 180° = 540°

(4) For 25-gon, n = 25, sum of the interior angles = (25 - 2) x 180° = 4140°

(5) For Octagon, n = 8, sum of the interior angles = (8 - 2) x 180° = 1080°

8.G.B.6 - Verifying the Pythagorean Theorem

Question No.	Answer	Detailed Explanation
1	D	$a^2+b^2=c^2$ cannot be changed to $a^2+c^2=b^2$.
2	C	$9^2+12^2=15^2$ $81+144=225$ $225=225$
3	A	$4^2+4^2=c^2$ $32 = c^2$ 5.7 in $\approx c$
4	10	You will fill the legs into the equation. So the equation will be $6^2 + 8^2 = c^2$. When you square both of those you get $100 = c^2$. To get c alone you have to take the square root of both sides. When you do this you have $\sqrt{100} = C$. So once you take the square root, you are left with $c = 10$.

8.G.B.7 - Pythagorean Theorem in Real-World Problems

Question No.	Answer	Detailed Explanation
1	B	$a^2+a^2=50^2$ $2a^2=2500$ $a^2=1250$; $a=35$ yd (approx)
2	A	$30^2+20^2=d^2$ $1300=d^2$ $\sqrt{1300}=d$; $d=$ approx. 36 ft
3	B	$20^2+15^2=d^2$ $625=d^2$ 25 ft$=d$ $20+15=35$ ft ; The diagonal would be 10 ft shorter.
4	(1) 10, 26 (2) 30 (3) 5, 11.2	(1) The first example you are looking for the other leg. Since the base length is 48, you have to cut it in half to make the right triangle. So in this case, one of the legs will be 24 cm.. The hypotenuse is going to be the slant height of 26 cm. This means you are solving for the other leg. When you fill the numbers into Pythagorean Theorem you get 10 cm. (2) The next example you have both a leg and a hypotenuse, so you are solving for the other leg. In this case the other leg will be 15 in. which is half of the base length. So, base length will be 30 in. (3) The last example you have both legs, 5 ft. and 10 ft. So the length of the ladder will be the hypotenuse. In this case it will be about 11.2 ft.

8.G.B.8 - Pythagorean Theorem & Coordinate System

Question No.	Answer	Detailed Explanation
1	C	$25+9=34=d^2$ $d=5.8$ (approximately)
2	C	$4^2+4^2=d^2$ $32=d^2$ $d=5.7$ (approximately)
3	B	$2^2+10^2=AB^2$ $\sqrt{104}=AB$ $10.2=AB$ (approximately) $4^2+9^2=AC^2$ $\sqrt{97}=AC$ $9.8=AC$ (approximately) Note that, we can conclude AB > AC without calculating square root also, because $AB^2>AC^2$ implies AB >AC

4

	10.8	12.2	13	14.8
(6, 5) and (-4, 9)	●	○	○	○
(-8, 0) and (5, -7)	○	○	○	●
(-4, -9) and (6, -2)	○	●	○	○
(5, 4) and (12, 15)	○	○	●	○

Distanace between two points having coordinates (x1,y1) and (x2,y2) can be found out with the help of Pythagorean Theorem. D= $\sqrt{(x2-x1)^2 + (y2-y1)^2}$. Using this formula we get -

(i) d = 10.8
(ii) d = 14.8
(iii) d = 12.2
(iv) d = 13

8.G.C.9 - Finding Volume: Cone, Cylinder, & Sphere

Question No.	Answer	Detailed Explanation
1	D	$V_{cylinder} = \pi r^2 h$ $V_{cone} = \frac{1}{3} \pi r^2 h$ If volumes are the same, then the height of the cone must be 3 times the height of the cylinder because $3(\frac{1}{3}) = 1$.
2	C	$V_{sphere} = \frac{4}{3} \pi r^3$ $V = \frac{4}{3}(8)\pi$ $V = \frac{32}{3}\pi$ $V_{cylinder} = \pi r^2 h$ $V = 8\pi$ $V_{cone} = \frac{1}{3} \pi r^2 h$ $V = (\frac{1}{3})(9)(4)\pi$ $V = 12\pi$; The cone has the greatest volume.
3	D	$V_{sphere} = \frac{4}{3} \pi r^3$ $V = \frac{4}{3}\pi(27)$ $V = 36\pi$ $V_{cylinder} = \pi r^2 h$ $V = 9(4)\pi$ $V = 36\pi$ $V_{cone} = \frac{1}{3} \pi r^2 h$ $V = (\frac{1}{3})(36)(3)\pi$ $V = 36\pi$
4	75.36 ft³	Radius of the cone = r = 3 ft. Height of the cone = h = 8 ft. Volume of the cone = V = (1/3) $\pi r^2 h$ V = (1/3) x 3.14 x 3² x 8 V = 75.36 ft³

Statistics and Probability

8.SP.A.1 Interpreting Data Tables & Scatter Plots

1. Data for 9 kids' History and English grades are made available in the chart. What is the association between the History and English grades?

Kids	1	2	3	4	5	6	7	8	9
History	63	49	84	33	55	23	71	62	41
English	67	69	82	32	59	26	73	62	39

Ⓐ Positive association
Ⓑ Negative association
Ⓒ Nonlinear association
Ⓓ Constant association

2. Data for 9 kids' History grades and the distance they live from school are made available in the chart. What is the association between these two categories?

Kids	1	2	3	4	5	6	7	8	9
History	63	49	84	33	55	23	71	62	41
Distance from School (miles)	.5	7	3	4	5	2	3	6	9

Ⓐ No association
Ⓑ Positive association
Ⓒ Negative association
Ⓓ Constant association

3. Data for 9 kids' Math and Science grades are made available in the chart. What is the association between the Math and Science grades?

Kids	1	2	3	4	5	6	7	8	9
Science	63	49	84	33	55	23	71	62	41
Math	67	69	82	32	59	26	73	62	39

Ⓐ Positive association
Ⓑ No association
Ⓒ Constant association
Ⓓ Negative association

4. **Following is 10 days of data which shows the sale of apples and mangoes. Fill in the type of association there is between the apple and mango sales.**

Days	1	2	3	4	5	6	7	8	9	10
Apple	62	49	81	26	45	55	16	74	97	34
Mango	36	44	49	37	26	11	76	83	64	81

There is [   ] between apple and mango sale

8.SP.A.2 Scatter Plots, Line of Best Fit

1. Which scatter plot represents a positive linear association?

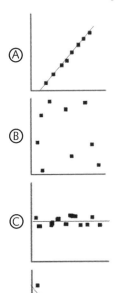

2. Which scatter plot represents a negative linear association?

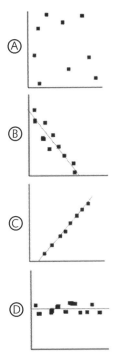

3. **Which scatter plot represents no association?**

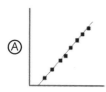
Ⓐ

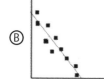
Ⓑ

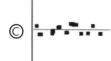
Ⓒ

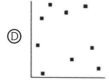
Ⓓ

4. **Cathy wanted to know what kind of shows the 8th grade class preferred – dramas or comedies. 55 students said they liked comedies and not dramas. 25 students liked both dramas and comedies. There were 41 students who did not like dramas nor comedies. Complete a two way table using the information given.**

	Doesn't Like Dramas	Likes Dramas	Total
Doesn't Like Comedies	41		97
Likes Comedies		25	
Total	96		177

8.SP.A.3 Analyzing Linear Scatter Plots

1. The figure below shows a scatter plot relating the length of a bean plant, in centimeters, to the number of days since it was planted. The slope of the associated line is 2. Which of the following correctly interprets the slope?

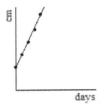

Ⓐ The bean plant grows approximately 1 cm every 2 days.
Ⓑ The bean plant grows approximately 2 cm each day.
Ⓒ The bean plant was 2 cm long when it was planted.
Ⓓ The bean plant approximately doubles in length each day.

2. The figure below shows a scatter plot relating the cost of a ride in a taxicab, in dollars, to the number of miles traveled. The slope of the associated line is 0.5. Which of the following correctly interprets the slope?

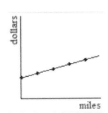

Ⓐ For each additional mile traveled, the cost of the ride increases by 50 cents.
Ⓑ For each additional half of a mile traveled, the cost of the ride increases by 1 dollar.
Ⓒ The initial cost of the ride, before the taxi has traveled any distance, is 50 cents.
Ⓓ The first half of a mile does not cost anything.

3. The figure below shows a scatter plot relating the temperature in a school's parking lot, in degrees Fahrenheit, to the number of hours past noon. The slope of the associated line is -3. Which of the following correctly interprets the slope?

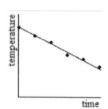

Ⓐ The temperature at noon was -3 degrees Fahrenheit.
Ⓑ The temperature decreased until it reached -3 degrees Fahrenheit.
Ⓒ The temperature decreased an average of 1 degree Fahrenheit every 3 hours.
Ⓓ The temperature decreased an average of 3 degrees Fahrenheit per hour.

4. Match the correct vocab term with the correct definition.

	Linear	Negative Association	Line of Best Fit	Prediction Equation
A line on a graph showing the general direction that a group of points seem to be heading	○	○	○	○
A graph that is represented by a straight line	○	○	○	○
The equation of a line that can predict outcomes using given data	○	○	○	○
A correlation of points that is linear with a negative slope	○	○	○	○

8.SP.A.4 Relatable Data Frequency

1.

	Fertilizer	No Fertilizer
Lived	200	600
Died	50	150

Out of 1,000 plants, some were given a new fertilizer and the rest were given no fertilizer. Some of the plants lived and some of them died, as shown in the table above. Which of the following statements is supported by the data?

Ⓐ Fertilized plants died at a higher rate than unfertilized plants did.
Ⓑ Fertilized plants and unfertilized plants died at the same rate.
Ⓒ Fertilized plants died at a lower rate than unfertilized plants died.
Ⓓ None of the above statements can be supported by the data.

2.

	Windy	Not Windy
Sunny	5	15
Cloudy	4	6

The weather was observed for 30 days; each day was classified as sunny or cloudy, and also classified as windy or not windy. The results are shown in the table above. Which of the following statements is NOT supported by the data?

Ⓐ 25% of the sunny days were also windy.
Ⓑ 30% of the days were windy.
Ⓒ 40% of the cloudy days were also windy.
Ⓓ 50% of the windy days were also sunny.

3.

	Jeans	No Jeans
Sneakers	15	10
No Sneakers	5	20

50 people were asked whether they were wearing jeans and whether they were wearing sneakers. The results are shown in the table above.

What fraction of the people who wore sneakers were NOT wearing jeans?

Ⓐ $\frac{1}{5}$

Ⓑ $\frac{2}{5}$

Ⓒ $\frac{3}{10}$

Ⓓ $\frac{3}{4}$

4. June surveyed the 7th and 8th grades to see which class they liked better, math or English. The results are shown in the two-way table below. Answer the question that follows.

	Math	English
7ᵗʰ grade	78	67
8ᵗʰ grade	86	45

The relative frequency of 7th grade students that chose math to all 7th grade students is _____

Statistics and Probability

Answer Key
&
Detailed Explanations

8.SP.A.1 - Interpreting Data Tables & Scatter Plots

Question No.	Answer	Detailed Explanation
1	A	As the History grade increases, so does the English grade. Thus, there is a positive association.
2	A	There does not appear to be any significant correlation between these two variables.
3	A	As the Science grade increases, so does the Math grade. This indicates a positive association.
4	no association	There is no association between the apple and mango sales. You can see that they neither consistently go up or go down over the course of the 10 days.

8.SP.A.2 - Scatter Plots, Line of Best Fit

Question No.	Answer	Detailed Explanation
1	A	The first scatter plot shows a positive slope representing a positive linear association.
2	B	The second scatter plot shows a negative slope representing a negative linear association.
3	D	The data on the fourth scatter plot cannot be represented linearly and, therefore, represents no association.
4	(1) 56 (2) 55, 80 (3) 81	*see table and explanation below*

	Doesn't Like Dramas	Likes Dramas	Total
Doesn't Like Comedies	41	56	97
Likes Comedies	55	25	80
Total	96	81	177

To solve how many like dramas and doesn't like comedies, you could take 97 - 41 to get 56. Next you know that 55 liked comedies but not dramas. To get the total number of students who liked comedies, just add 55 + 25 to get 80. Lastly to get the total of how many like dramas, take 56 + 25 to get 81.

8.SP.A.3 - Analyzing Linear Scatter Plots

Question No.	Answer	Detailed Explanation
1	B	We are told that the slope is 2. The slope is always the change on the vertical axis divided by the change on the horizontal axis; so a slope of 2 would be interpreted as 2/1 which represents 2 units on the vertical axis for every unit on the horizontal axis. Looking at the graph we see that the vertical axis is cm and the horizontal axis is days. Therefore a slope of 2=2/1 would represent 2 cm growth for each day.
2	A	Slope represents the (change on the vertical axis) / (the change on the horizontal axis). The vertical axis represents dollars and the horizontal axis represents miles; so a slope of 0.5 would be interpreted as 0.5 dollars per mile or 0.5 dollars/mile which is 50 cents for each mile traveled.
3	D	We are told that the graph relates the temperature in a school's parking lot, in degrees Fahrenheit, to the number of hours past noon. A slope of -3/1 = a temperature decrease of 3°F/hour.

Question No. 4

	Linear	Negative Association	Line of Best Fit	Prediction Equation
A line on a graph showing the general direction that a group of points seem to be heading	○	○	●	○
A graph that is represented by a straight line	●	○	○	○
The equation of a line that can predict outcomes using given data	○	○	○	●
A correlation of points that is linear with a negative slope	○	●	○	○

The line that is on the graph that doesn't necessarily go through every point but represents the general trend of the graph would be the line of best fit. If it is a straight line, then it is a linear graph. The equation of the best fit line that helps you predict outcomes are the prediction equation. Lastly, if the trend of the scatter plot has a negative slope then it has a negative association.

8.SP.A.4 - Relatable Data Frequency

Question No.	Answer	Detailed Explanation
1	B	Fertilized plants: $\frac{50}{200} = \frac{1}{4}$ died Unfertilized plants: $\frac{150}{600} = \frac{1}{4}$ died **They died at the same rate is the correct choice.**
2	D	There were a total of 9 windy days and 5 of them were also sunny. $\frac{5}{9} = 56\%$ The correct choice is 50% of the windy days were also sunny.
3	B	Out of 25 people wearing sneakers, 10 were not wearing jeans. $\frac{10}{25} = \frac{2}{5}$ $\frac{2}{5}$ is the correct answer.
4	0.54	To get the relative frequency you will take the number of 7th grade students that chose math and divide it by the total number of 7th graders. In this case you will take 78 and divide it by 145. When you do this, you get 0.54 (when rounded to the nearest hundredth).

Additional Information

What if I buy more than one Lumos Study Program?

Step 1

Visit the URL and login to your account.
http://www.lumoslearning.com

Step 2

Click on 'My tedBooks' under the "Account" tab.
Place the Book Access Code and submit.

Step 3

To add the new book for a registered student, choose the
◯ Existing Student button and select the student and submit.

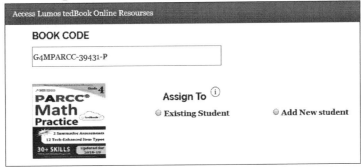

To add the new book for a new student, choose the ◯ Add New student
button and complete the student registration.

Lumos StepUp® Mobile App FAQ For Students

What is the Lumos StepUp® App?

It is a FREE application you can download onto your Android Smartphones, tablets, iPhones, and iPads.

What are the Benefits of the StepUp® App?

This mobile application gives convenient access to Practice Tests, Common Core State Standards, Online Workbooks, and learning resources through your Smartphone and tablet computers.
- Eleven Technology enhanced question types in both MATH and ELA
- Sample questions for Arithmetic drills
- Standard specific sample questions
- Instant access to the Common Core State Standards
- Jokes and cartoons to make learning fun!

Do I Need the StepUp® App to Access Online Workbooks?

No, you can access Lumos StepUp® Online Workbooks through a personal computer. The StepUp® app simply enhances your learning experience and allows you to conveniently access StepUp® Online Workbooks and additional resources through your smartphone or tablet.

How can I Download the App?

Visit **lumoslearning.com/a/stepup-app** using your Smartphone or tablet and follow the instructions to download the app.

QR Code
for Smartphone
Or Tablet Users

Lumos StepUp® Mobile App FAQ For Parents and Teachers

What is the Lumos StepUp® App?

It is a free app that teachers can use to easily access real-time student activity information as well as assign learning resources to students. Parents can also use it to easily access school-related information such as homework assigned by teachers and PTA meetings. It can be downloaded onto smartphones and tablets from popular App Stores.

What are the Benefits of the Lumos StepUp® App?

It provides convenient access to

- Standards aligned learning resources for your students
- An easy to use Dashboard
- Student progress reports
- Active and inactive students in your classroom
- Professional development information
- Educational Blogs

How can I Download the App?

Visit **lumoslearning.com/a/stepup-app** using your Smartphone or tablet and follow the instructions to download the app.

**QR Code
for Smartphone
Or Tablet Users**

Other Books By Lumos Learning For High School

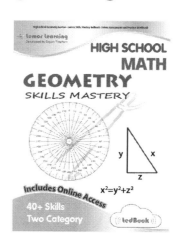

Available

- At Leading book stores
- www.lumoslearning.com/a/lumostedbooks

Made in the USA
Columbia, SC
29 August 2020